akal

Published in Great Britain in 2023
by Big White Shed, Morecambe
www.bigwhiteshed.co.uk
Printed and bound by Imprint Digital, Devon

ISBN 978-1-915021-19-9
Copyright © David Wood
Cover illustration by David Wood

A CIP catalogue record of this book is available from
the British Library.

seventy poems for seventy meditations

dedicated to

contents

introduction

Soon after the turn of the millennium, and to support a friend, I took up a specific kind of yoga: Kundalini; I felt (and still feel) each creak and crack, though I somehow developed enough of a rough and ready suppleness that helped me cope with too much time sitting in front of the computer. There were some weeks I took breaks due to time and/or economics; I always came back.

2020 meant face to face yoga had to go; in 2021, using the same tutor, I took up Kundalini meditation as a live, online session; this included hand mudhras, chanting and focussed breathing.

That same year, I gave myself a challenge: I would create a poem after each Thursday evening. The only regular reader was Denise, the Kundalini tutor.

akal (meaning: undying), is the result. Some reflect the meditation processes directly; other poems picked up on current personal situations including grief, mental and physical health and my absurd way of looking at life.

one - seed sow

we seed-sow – so what's below is strong
i am that which *is* - and happy then to be
how we build on the what we were – seek new songs
between our mantra – the mantra's in our creed

i am that which is - and happy then to be
sometimes we need remind ourselves (without – within)
strength works – rotates around our hands – feeds
and churns – life dances in its spin

how we build on the what we were – we seek new songs
we find our breath – it walks a heart shape land
slow the spin – eyes closed – vision's on
we know the prayer - time's sunshine – we are – i am

between the mantra – the mantra's in our creed
i am that which is and happy then to be

two - lotus flowers

we are lotus
we open
bring the petals
to our hearts

and by whatever wall
we find ourselves
we'll push against its mortar
know it will crumble soon

our voices know the song
much that we draw upon
we bring it into prayer
towards such stage of happiness

and we are happy
we are good
however fingers point at us
we laugh them off

we lock
we let it go

we lock against the world
and fire a cannon at the dark

we stretch

breath lets us be
and healed

then so

three - other

self-heal – healing selves
we move within our ways
hands shift - hand heat
hands out and
like a bird (palms down)
we are abacus

count
       the ins
       the holds
       the half second out

we wait

fathom vibration
we make (and made)
       odd angles

utter strange words

know things are better now
and send it out

i – you – them – other

four - the art of being very

very-ness in vulnerability
churning those out
on leaving delicate birds
to the harsh

very wordness
which is what
i've tried to say
nothing happening
until i make it

very meaning
lifting
dropping a spade
on hard soil

earth shudder

on very snowness snowing
feeling the lace curtains
grow dampness

feather
wet
soak

on being very falling

we know how the lifting strings work
someone snip snip snipping them
shapeless

on very being

i would choose the letter *g*
it is at the cliff side
waiting for the tide

on the very how

this is when the arms raise
palms parallel to the sky
in holdingness

baby pose
rock pose
supine twist

five - fulfil (the f-word)

whatever we mould (creative) between our hands –
earth – air – fire – wind – the emptiness no longer there
we hold something – a *thing* – we hold its elan
(its buzz) and close our eyes - somehow we see it clearer

palms face to – palms sing out - we carve such lines
and send potential to the way we need to be
we stir in tiny circles – our fingers making fine
marks into the shakes - we find out who we are – three

periods of two – three ways – three steps – holding
on to the f-word at the end – we are both sides – send
our applause – hips gnawing – the buzz thrumming
i am thine – in mine – myself – fulfilment

what this thing is and could also ever mean
energy becoming – being and between

six – landing mark

one clumsy foot in front
i fall towards my side
the balance in my centre line
has fallen down across the years

my head is full of butterfly
that's not quite mastered yet
(its wings start awkward
to the way the thoughts
have wandered off)

until

whatever happens in the head
is empty but for a simple humming
of the tongue

i'm told to seek a path
(though not sure where
or what it is)
i know it offers better songs
than this morning's dew
that worried out and wrapped me
in its wire

i lay path's first clumsy
cobble stone
and fix my frozen toes
so i can find my landing mark

i'm still not sure
(i am unsure)

but whatever ways
i dance inside tonight
i'll hope to find out
what my prayer
points to

vibration in my fingertips
lotus up above

saa re saa saa
saa re saa saarang

seven - hands

we clarify – build resilience – start with fire
spark each finger - we know exactly what to focus on
we field the differences – one holds the nine
one track's held by him that understands that higher

plane is lost to names like his for now (still he perseveres)
we pray hands up – the steeple-eye demands our sight
keeps its promise somehow strong – our forefinger
                                        (jupiter)
and its ego brings its airs and graces to the light

and gives us challenges to wrap our hands around
saturn (in the middle) helps somewhat – shares the
                                        strength
listens to the way - we share out the lengths
we dig our heels into – earth and sun have found

us like we knew they would – so mercury and water –
                                        fluid into air
we break what shadows cast – and negative (simply)
                                        disappears

eight - wringing

we wring ourselves free – in comes out
out's no longer in – we are creative
we chip away - some kind of detritus
packs its bags and waves goodbye

how odd
we do this
through the
holding of
some offbeat
angle
and the placing
of our hands

we lean towards the wind
and stop before we forward fall

we are with balance
we are unblocked

we will rest
we will invent

we will know

nine - wrestle

i am
       in waking

i am
arms crossing
pumping

(i am brief pained)

i am
       battle drawn
       aching
             truth finding

i am several points of eight
i am not holding

i am

my stomach
tells me

pull in

i am steps towards

i am hurt-struggle

i am combative

i am full with

i am with roots

open

i am in become
i am self

true

what i am

ten - build

whatever bricks we yield inside
(whatever mortar
churned into the mix)

we continue to build towards
       the halting of the dark
       the growling of the teeth
       the falling off the cliff
       the keeping of secrets
       the standstill
       the fading out button

in the spirit of radiance
we have saved enough
to put something
back
for such moments
of un-balance

in our universe
spring knows its way out
doors opening both ways

and us pushing
against the wind

eleven - clearance
(making the impossible – possible)

inner voice
deep shit
between the waves
dark fits

chant clear
light seams
sleep deep
seek dreams

so then
now we
vibrate
again

dawn face
like the sun
impossible
then begun

twelve - how to deal with the sea

i heard the sea –
felt it with its monkey mind
– legs fast pacing
told it to leave me be –
i was already listening
to the sound of the sea

the sea was all in -
nobody wanted it
on their sandwiches
or in their fizzy drinks

we took it to the roofs of our mouths
and pointed to many ways
it could deal with itself

do yourself a favour – sea
we held our exclamation
for as long as we could

crossing and pressing
and tapping and shifting
concentrating
putting the sea into
a thumbnail sketch
of its former self

when the sea
shakes you
to the skin

make it a song
and join on in

thirteen - the big red clumsy bus

i say goodbye to
i throw over my shoulder
i flick away

whatever ties me to my habits
whatever drowns me sometimes
whatever waves of obsession i carry
                in my bone brittle bag

whateverfallsmeovermyselfwhilei'mstillrunning

whatever i lean back on
when the heat brings itself to me
like a big red clumsy bus

whatever behaviour i adopt to muddle through
whatever i pretend to be when i am not

i say goodbye to
i throw over my shoulder
i flick away

i know the way i become
my body learned it
my wires kicked in

i fall back upon
i am sometimes
i am always
i am ever

say goodbye - pain

over my shoulder - pain
flick away – pain

new patterns
life lift
outward – seeing

fourteen - footsteps on our tongues

today i ache – my fingernails full of earth's garden
                                         richness
my shoulders carry me through and my jokes as bad as
                                         they come
and now i seek to measure how i am – check in with
                                         myself
copy the moves – take the numbers and throw them to
                                         the evening light

the moon breathes later (lighter) now – birdsong constant
                                  – i try to con-cen-trate
and find the struggle with my own clumsy way – i blame
                                         my tiredness
as if it was another part of myself – we wear our eyes –
                                         see between
what's not been glimpsed before – we roll our positivity –
                                         push into

our mouths and find the footsteps on our tongues – not a
                                         march but
electricity of some *ether* kind – our palate returns to us -
                                         silence
elbows out the voices' speak (let's do this – let's do that –
                                     let's do something else)
i know the practice does me good – it works invisible –
                                         cups me in its ways

and by the final prayer – this tune's a welcome guest
thinking's put away for now - mind's at rest at rest at rest

fifteen - dance contentment

what we seek — we sit -
we know contentment
has the content in its grasp
we ready into our ways
and find three paths

heart silent
hush quiet
loud speak out

we consider
what liminal beat
what space we
move into

sometimes i do not understand
where genuine peace comes from
where i go to
dropping off strange cliffs
and bouncing in the sea

how stillness walks with some
and not with others

what strange clouds
i keep
and how it rains
in colour

sixteen - the wrench (a prayer)

give me inside – make the *isn't* – *is*
cure me of tiredness – tell me the way i may
wake the outside – stop the rage
when i'm in this state

here comes the magic three again

heart
stomach
head

i bring the prayer to my self
and let the rain above me
drop it gentle where i sit

give me the wrench to prise
the wakefulness from out its shell

hand on heart – vibration steals me in
i know the day's length of to and fro
                has eaten me
like the monster that i am

still - i enjoy the pulse of this time
within myself

i talk of strength
i hope for its touch
know its theory
find it difficult
to coax it out

sometimes it's like a willing dog
coming with a whistle

other days
i need to deliberate

real hard
always further on

seventeen - an attempt at fixing

nothing's smooth – pain rakes across these shoulders
the body screams – i scrape at weakened gaps
i'm cursing at myself - my back – what boulders
shift on top of me - adds weight to where i'm sat

the body screams – i scrape at weakened gaps
i'm in resentment – what makes me carry on
is knowing that i fall too easy – (i wear its dark cloud hat)
i grit and swear beneath my breath – i'll soon be done

i'm cursing at myself - my back – what boulders
rolled like sisyphus up some steep hill
are counteractions to my slackness – my doldrums
i've lived with this past year (swallowed) like a sugar pill

now this damn strain shifts on top of me - adds weight to
                                        where i'm sat
the body screams - you bugger! i scrape at weakened gaps

eighteen - cough

we are in quadrant
dream state and otherwise

sometimes my mind is twisted
sometimes it relies on my tongue
to form the letters that i need

that too
follows a clumpy path

i call the wrong name
i make something abstract
out of something clear cut

we are in quadrant

we try coughing out the air
making the letter *aitch*
with the backs of our throats

we hope for better days
typing our lives out
in odd poetic chant-wise

without even knowing
what the last line will be

quadrant indeed

nineteen - me

i am all hands and feet
and thoughts tonight

each time i shift
that between-ness
the gap

the silent sweep
of one hand
two

i sense the words
shifting on
clawing
telling me
speaking through me
holding on to
me

i turn away
turn back

my revolution
in finding where
strength keeps
burning

i know several thousand ways to do this
as many as there are gates inside

opening
closing

opening
closing

breathing
namaste

twenty - happiness blossom difficulty

too busy for happiness – days are way long
nights split in too short a sequence
too buzzing – the body grows round corners
and the words that are given
know they pose a trial by sitting in stillness

i keep trying -
happiness and honesty – odd bedfellows
one grabs the duvet
the other rolls over and falls flat
on his own shortcomings
(disturbing the blossom)

my fingers misbehave
my words lose the meditation
i keep trying

i'm being honest
        i guess

(no red noses on this poem's face)
which makes me happy

sat nam
wahe guru

twenty one - count

each finger makes me
points me
counts me
confuses me

damn my laboured breath
and further damn
the slowness
of my stupid self

it is like my wi-fi
sometimes stalking me
in the backwoods
stopping halfway on the moon
and making the impossible
             possible

i know where i try to lead myself
but i overthink
think over too much

the flow is there
all i need is the waking up
the vision of the way through
(the eyes shuffle uncomfortably here)

the gladness dreams of all it can
and settles in the long grass

twenty two – wrings

non-drift
whatever it is
(or isn't)
tells me
over
over

back to the beat

then i shift

each flavour
of wrong
wrings its hands
tells its song
blows its nose
finds its way in
i hit it round the chops
with a quiet prayer
i am always grateful for

twenty three - doubt

this life thing
this breathing thing
this song thing

i try my best

i'm never sure
where i'm going with it

this life stuff
this breathing stuff
this song stuff

i find myself doubting

and always like a broken gate
talking to its hinges
(rusted to the nines)

this life is
this breathing remains
this song sings

i dig in
i keep hoping
it will drop on me somehow

this life
this breathing
this song

twenty four - getting used

it all takes time

i remind myself
peace enters
bit by bit

(we can't chew the future
            all at once)
we hold ourselves to account
stare inside ourselves
break our own shadows
pull ourselves up

it all takes time
section by section
breath by breath
(by breath)

we know the gaps
we feel the clumsiness
tonight

i am not used to this
    -    this wellness

            the being
            is still becoming

god knows i try

sometimes i make a joke
to get through it all

sometimes not

sometimes i stare above me
always something higher
much higher
much - much higher

time - yeah right

twenty five - the world working (river flow)

despite or
because of the rain

finally the world sits
between our thumbs

we wash the world
like a river
on a forty degree spin
we give it space
we call out its name

(it has different names
which we won't go into
as these may offend
or twist the tongue
too quickly)

feeling better
the window is open
the falling of water has ceased
being what it was

i am sitting on my duvet
calling out daft words
like everyone else

i'd like them to be

bus stop
sponge cake
candle wax

but they're not

and it doesn't matter

bus stop
sponge cake
candle wax

twenty six - peach

open me
prise me
split with your mantra
look into me
tip me up and count the pieces

shake the box
dream me sideways
bring me back inside myself
and make me focus

like a soft peach

open me
the flesh is mine
(i'll share the melody
somehow)

now heal me

tell me what to say
over
over
over
and heal me
with my own concentration

stop me drifting
bring me into the room again

i know its blessing
and exactly what it does

twenty seven - continuum

what colour is the infinite?
which colour takes me to continuum?

when the circle wheels
towards the waves
what sea gives me strength
rolls me - helps me seek again?

what colour is that sea?
what shape is that cloud tumbling into change?

some know it by heart
i have to learn its lines
by water mark

dry myself off

twenty eight – ham sandwich

shabba dabba
shabba dabba
shabba dabbity daaaah

[say it]

blah blah blah
oooom gaaaaa
gaaadidy gaaah
gaaah gaaaah

[raise your hands
cross the thumb over itself
    -    sing the next one]

grum dee bubbly dah
[slowly and from the third eye]

hang out your bra bra brah

ha ha
ham sandwich

[tuck your feet under your shoulders]

urgh eurgh ongh

hands together
prayer pose
shine your light
namaste

twenty nine – purity acrostics

perhaps the 'i' wades into the depths
understanding nothing (at least - not in the seekingness)
right - let's get a move on -
i (or the eye) finds itself loosened up
this meaning the other – at least sleep is gifted towards
you – your dreams – your clarity – your less-ness-less

which point of meaning is sleep?
it is in the centre of i and the gift of the you
i make a song and send it (in a shake) to your
dark moments (turning to gladioli
on a bright window—sill) – my advice - keep it
safe – let it have its way

thirty - abundance

cup me with abundance
in small things

peace of mind
a big crazy smile
two vegetarian sausages

harree harree

bring my soul into ways
of seeing

light when i need it
sorrow when it shows itself
two slices of toast

find me my way through
dense forests of the mind
pathways to other places
the café on the corner

tell me what i need to process
how to be with dyspraxia
laughter – how it is needed

the cooking of an egg
without breaking its yolk

and don't tell the vegans

thirty one - dealing with it

i will it so
i am not angry
i have no turbulence
it is in abeyance

otherways
i give in
become the colour red
-      the blood rush
           will not sit still

it is in a furious alphabet
there is no control
and the roughshod way
drags me by the soles of my feet

i draw it
(inside myself)
like a small clot
of electricity

the dot is a target

i see it
i step inside
make myself a drawbridge

sometimes it's up
other times – shamefacedly open
letting in the bloodlust
pulling at its sword

thirty two - will tell you

between meditation practice
and the poem
i indulge myself
with the cycles of female song

kate bush
edie brickell
tracey thorn

the poem will tell you of a dance in the throat
the poem will tell you of our hand movements
the poem will describe utterances
why they matter
what they do
what they give us

what stuff they release

sometimes i sit
and wonder what i am doing

my arms rotating
my hand on my heart
wild callings in myself

thirty three - russian dolls

so this is me
inside the many russian dolls
one skin nudges the other
one thought screams to get out
another lurches sideways
one breakage leads to many
(all breakages must be paid for)

still me then
several stacking crates in a pile
a hand inside a larger one
the gasp in a cloud
bounces back
hurts the fabric of this place

always me
picking up pieces
and pieces for the pickings
the layers i'm aware of
the layers i wait for

the russian doll
a hand
a cloud

a joke when needs be

myself staring
- outside in
inside out

self-fabric

thirty four - a folk song to the lungs

arms up – fingers spread
wake up – yer bugger-o!
breathe in – breathe out
time to take control-eeoo

fall out – fall in
round and round the lungs it goes
sing on – song flow
one minute to go you know

pain come - pain blow
focus on the centre-o
lie down – fall back
make like a corpse-ee-o

time done – time gone
don't forget the prayer-ee-o
no - don't forget the prayer-ee-o
no - don't forget the prayer-ee-o
[repeat until fade-ee-o]

thirty five - too many

the world begins
with pointing

one hand accused the other
you are lazy
good for nothing
an open parenthesis

one prepares the dark
the other sings a song
colours up a joke

i will write
my goodbye days
to many long friends

my head asks
how many more to go?

i have tried being an angel
i have tried being a god

i point upwards
i point towards

inside is the tricky one

thirty six - drowse throughout

i throw out my non-sleep
inside i am sleeping
inside is my dream
i throw it out

i wonder if my dream
is sleeping
i am inside a drowse
i throw it out

inside my dream
i find the dark thing
this is sleeping
i throw it out

where do i keep my dream
with my dark thing?
it is in my way
i throw it out

we are made of dream
who doesn't have dark thing?
thing that sleep
we throw it out

it want to stay
sleep drowse dark thing
things i ask
thing throwing out

thirty seven - teach

teach me patience – teach me sight
somewhere wander hold my hand
teach me somehow – teach me night
here in blindness – glass from sand

here in blindness – glass from sand
teach me somehow – teach me night
somewhere wander hold my hand –
teach me patience – teach me sight

teach me somehow – teach me night
here in blindness – glass from sand
teach me somehow – teach me night
teach me patience – teach me sight

somewhere wander hold my hand –
teach me patience – teach me sight
here in blindness – glass from sand
teach me somehow – teach me night

thirty eight - of myself

call me restless – discover my beat
my time sat down
rings too many circles

i cannot be at peace
i am at pieces of myself

calm me breathless – i chase my breathing
my breathing chases me - drops me
where it wishes – formless
always – wishing for stillness

hold me deepness – offer me exact
pinpoint me somehow – draw me linear
i have become no one's dance
and scattered like powder on the wrong floor

thirty nine - position

between autumn waves
i kick myself to a dark pavement
i have held the wrong type of water
time knows this
goes to bed with such
a cold mantra
(is comforted by it)

and i am aware of
the child
from the *in*
making its scream
to the *out*

whatever i say now
i wear old habits
muscle memories
finely tuned songs
bad chorus'

i practise

i hold out my hand
take a new cloud

catch a strange rain
shift into other ways
tell a new position

lie down
sit up
state my prayer

guide my way on

forty - solutions

the hands feel where the crisis starts
the hands lift in the tender grip
the hands take the waves apart
the hands shift – the hands slip

the hands *are* – the hands belong
the hands seal the heart in strength
the hands wake the spirit song
the hands' width - the hands' length

the hands weave – the pain's less
the hands contain - the fingers point
the hands cup – the hands' nest
the hands wash – the song anoints

all hands pray – all mouths bless
night comes into our eyes – we rest

forty one - bum

hummy hum
bra hum
hummy hum
bra hum

tummy trump
bra bump
tummy trump
bra bump

runny bum
fart hump
runny bum
fart hump

[don't lose it]

sunny gum
tart rump
sunny gum
tart rump

bunny grump
bar chump
bunny grump
bar chump

[concentrate on your third eye]

funny lump
chomp chomp
funny lump

chomp chomp

rub your bum
tiddly tum
rub your bum
tiddly tum

by 'eck
wahey wahey
phwoar gnu

bless you

forty two - courage - be yourself

sa-ta-na-ma

which is hard when
the woman
throws numbers at me
and they bounce
across me like knives

things i need to remember
and quickly forget

har har har hari

and i'm trying to
remember what she said
and i'm making a joke of it
(bullets over my head)

wahe guru

and i'm trying to work out
what she said
and what i need to understand
and how tearful i have become

just being there
at the opticians
and trying to see

sometimes i forget to breathe
or count

one – two – three – four
i am very strong

forty three - the fear of silence

when the song's inside and the lyrics change
the voices weave me to a labyrinth – shake the path
i know silence is never easy – it goes against my grain
to charge myself with nothing – when nothing is a gas

the voices weave me to a labyrinth – shake the path
i lose another friend – i can't sit still
tonight – i separate the frames – slot in the photographs
i know i should have strength – i know the drill

still i know silence isn't easy – it's poison to the grain
how many more to test the system? mark my score
send it to my thoughtfulness – label it with pain
bring voices to the maze – i'll chase them ever more

i charge myself with nothing – nothing leaves its gas
your voice weaves me to a labyrinth – shakes the path

forty four - new year 2022 - something dances

in my small room – i have my small voice
in my head – i have begun to bring the waves in
in my waves – the hands wash me with some odd song
in my odd song – my arms move – my fingers point

by my fingers – i stir up hope – like a shower of peace
with my shower of peace – i turn it to a resonance
my resonance falls sometimes when the thoughts come in
my thoughts are not welcome –
                              not at this moment anyway

inside my thoughts – i dodge the bullets
inside the bullets – i work out the metaphor
inside the metaphor – something dances
inside the dance – the small voice chirrups like a bird

forty five - we are: haiku

we will blossom now
when song is complete – we are
synchronicity

forty six - map

these are the maps in my hands —
and i'm no longer sure what they do

these are the lines of my hands
some of the lines are deep

what do i keep in my hands?
the history of where i have been

sometimes my hands are like windmills
sometimes they are like the blind

sometimes — they ask too many questions
there are times — i wish they would go away

my hands press buttons — turn dials - cook
wade in — squeeze too hard — knock things over

i forget the maps of my hands — sometimes
it's good to remind myself of where i am

i am not very good at navigation — my hands
lose themselves — each finger like a wick

and doused into the sea — my hands curl
round and produce a bowl of prayer

will i be?
shall i be?

let me be

forty seven - my inside room

we are odd balloons
at an even stranger party

one end shines
reflects the window light
one end is tied
to keep the magic in

and we are batteries
we let it out

we are ourselves
whatever we do
however we use our own calling
however we break the air

this is the way we pay it all back

tonight – my mind threw things around my inside room
        made a mess of it
        when it could have made peace

my concentration flew like smoke
in solid lumps

at least
i know whatever i took in
i sent towards

i'm hoping it helps
more than indeed

forty eight - can be - can't be - honestly

sometimes i resent this time
this time out to energise
to rejuvenate
to be what i can be

i fall asleep

and i'm already
resenting myself
for holding up my arms
for using those man-tras

for doing those tra-la-las

tra-la-laaaaaaaaaas

forty nine - time repeats time

am i too old for time? i pull it in and utter out
whatever things i find in there - repeat – repeat
we are equal then in life – but death has doubts
to when we go – make do – keep going – beat

out its lines – keep feeling time – and utter out
whatever fears you sit upon and hold too tight
towards your heart – we've spoke aloud
the names of those who've gone – the light

takes all of us in time – (death has its doubts)
keep breathing – keep holding – drawing in
be ready to let go when it's your time – shout
somehow – whatever matter you can a pin

inside – make it worth its while – don't be beat
whatever stuff you find in life - repeat – repeat

fifty - staunch the flow

butterfly – my hands inside – i clap the air
we listen for the trap of what we know
we believe ourselves – we concentrate – what's here
is what we struggle with – enters in then goes

we listen for the trap of what we know
i never keep the focus – still i'm still
my tongue lifts – drops – it's tough to staunch the flow
my negative creeps like a darkness in the mill

we trust ourselves – we are *distillate* – we're here
to work on what we can – silence in the throat
moves me – shifts me – stops me – keep me near
and then the meaning loses me inside its coat

we are what we struggle with – what enters in soon goes
we listen for the trap of what we know

fifty one - jupiter - saturn - sun - mercury

the universe proves heavy enough sometimes
jupiter saturn sun mercury in my hands
i look for symbols – count the signs

i'm pressing fingers – down the line
thumb's my ego – and where it lands
i find the universe is heavy sometimes

i crave my peace – for peace i'll ride
upon the back of stilling sands
with finding symbols – counting signs

i have lain back – for i'll abide
with what i sow – the way has plans
though universe is far too much sometimes

but i'll trust in what it gives – my eyes
are closed and concentrate – what wands
that give me symbols – show me signs

of how to operate in this place and time
i wish that there was magic in the can
for universe weighs too heavy sometimes
(constancy in symbol – counting signs)

fifty two - all i ask is to be superman

which way to fall
when to rise
how to stop
if i can
who i am
what to breathe
questions to ask
stones to break
time to fill
paths to feel
things to know
waves to catch
oceans to wade into
drawers to open
falling to get up

fifty three - that one

i am thinking too much
i am thinking without clarity
i am thinking without
i am thinking within

i am thinking about healing
i am thinking about grief
sometimes i don't know if i'm grieving
sometimes i feel it all over me

i am thinking about sunshine
sometimes this is difficult
sometimes i am in an awkward place
sometimes i fall over

i have swallowed dynamite
and wait for it to go bang
sometimes it goes pop
sometimes it lets go

i struggle keeping still
i struggle making things happen
my mate went away
and left big memories of him

sometimes we drank coffee
sometimes we drank tea

fifty four - the time's not right

i've been given a slice of silence i did not want
my go-to friend of eighteen years or so has gone
tonight my letter h (of quiet breath) helps me on
towards my own piece of thursday night

my go-to friend of eighteen years or so has gone
across some river of metaphor – some odd
shift within me awaits outburst - none
       comes – the time's not right

tonight my letter h (of quiet breath) helps me on
i find myself rocking the beats of the mantra run
until i'm sore with trying not to think again
       considering the light

i'm towards my own piece of thursday night
       considering the light
grief will come – the time's not right

fifty five - repeat

you need to dis-attach
you need to say this
you need to move

repeat repeat repeat

i need to know the sun
you need to move towards
you need to smile

repeat repeat repeat

you need to find the strength
i need to feel the shift
you need to vibrate

repeat repeat repeat

you need to greet the day
i need to concentrate
i need to make this work

repeat repeat repeat

i have noticed the elder
growing through the hedge
i have felt the warm wind
i have felt the cold wind

i have seen my failings
i know what to keep

repeat repeat repeat

fifty six - open box

we bring our own pain
i bring my own pain
you bring your own pain

there is no pain
there was no pain
there shall be no pain

pain will not be sought
we will not be with pain
we bring no pain

how is pain given?
it is given by us
in an open box

how is pain taken?
it is taken by us
from an open box

we lean forwards
we lean backwards
we call outside
we call inside

there is no pain
there was no pain
there shall be no pain

we are us
i am myself
in joy

amen

fifty seven - chunter

inside my babble again

whatever my outer voice speaks
my inner tongues keep
chuntering away

whatever my movements call me to
my taking in of air takes in too much
of the world again

i keep working
i keep bringing
i keep saying
i keep talking
i keep releasing

i am listening

instructions fall in
instructions fall out

i wrap myself in hope
sometimes i unravel
sometimes i am full of laughter
sometimes i am

fifty eight - like a church

i am already drifting
body heavy
body unhealed
mind splintered
paths being manifold
paths being trod

i am already trying
hands like a church
arms like a steam engine
head catching on

sometimes life is dark
sometimes it is not

i begin to wonder
when the light
creeps in
and what comes next

fifty nine - said

look not look
search not search
blind not blind
see not see
i not i
find not find
be not be

heal not heal
thee not thee
hurt not hurt
we not we

through our fingers – straight ahead
listen to what spirit said

sixty - beheld

i'll look for beauty then – seek the infinite
inside whatever breeze - we trade our gasps
we are like pylons – electricity is passed
between the points of energy – we contact

whatever light we shift – we trade our gasps
for what we can call ourselves – above our heads
we send protection (like umbrellas) instead
of letting in the darkness drawing down like shafts

beheld like pylons – where electricity is passed
we believe – we convince – we repeat 'til fade
and spring is like a doorway to the summer haze
that's still to come – we know whatever's waylaid

will work out these points of energy – these contacts
are our finger tips – beauty in their grasp

sixty one - there is

there is that hill – that test of me
that brings out the very thorns of me
that rolls me in its territory
that prods me with my name

there is that weight – i've carried it
for all my life i've married it
it seems too much – i've buried it
it's always looked the same

there is that way – a different path
where my feet have signed their autograph
to break the fence – to break the task
i question myself day by day

there is that doubt – i always keep
i know the answer's buried deep
sometimes i struggle – then i leap
there's bridges ahead yet to jump

what wonder lives inside the cage
's forgotten how to break its rage
i sit still – strength becomes its sage
still waiting for wisdom to show

sixty two - zoom-breath

two-night's breathing
will be interrupted by
glitches in the system
auto
aut o didact
d o th   iiiiiii ssss

tonight's arm movements
will be frozen in digital time

like theeeees

[your call is veeeeeery impooooortanttttttttt to ussssssss]

tonight my fists
my leg ga ga ga
w#will shake
rotate
waggle
at zzzzoom ma

#mama ma maaa maaa

tonight ta ta ta ta ta
my inner zzzzzelf
my psycheeeeee

79

will be mis-repaired
re-entangled
doused in pixel pix pix pie

sometimes i wonder at
the wurrrr   llllll   dddda da d
according to computers

it stops me breathing

sixty three - un

unlock me – unblock me – un-tell life
unfold me – decode me – pull me to one side
play me – delay me – take me for a ride

catch me – unlatch me – watch me rise
do you what you can – show me light
breathe me – keep me – day and night

move me – shift me – like the tide
do it all for me and energise
do it all for me and energise
do it all for me and energise
do it all for me and energise
do it all for me and energise
do it all for me and energise
do it all for me and energise
do it all for me and energise
do it all for me and energise
do it all for me and energise
do it all for me and energise
do it all for me and energise

sixty four - trying

i do the right things
the words tumble out in
easy to use moments
i do my best

why does the black dog
keep barking?

i speak when i can
break up my breaths
convince myself and others
all is good –
reasons do not matter

why does the black dog make
        such a noise
        while i'm thinking?

i eat the colours i need to
inside i will be a rainbow
i tell myself
be good to myself

why does the black dog
        make circles on my road?

i open doors
i carry the right smile
it fits me
it fits others
it makes jokes

why does the black dog
        bring the wrong boxes to my door?

sat nam
brah um
etc etc

sixty five - on happiness

where do i start?
where shall i start?

the root of happiness
is finding happiness

if you can't find happiness
you will become unhappy

what happens when you can find it?

you say *ha-ha*

what happens when you
try to find happiness?

when you screw up your face
you open your eyes
        your heart
you wade in open lakes
and talk to the water

what if the water isn't happiness?

what if the strains you make
the faces you pull
the dialogues you create
the creativity you well from out the bag
the endless coffee and cake
don't bring happiness

you say *ha-ha*
something happens
and breathing inside

sixty six - of me

we saw art today
drank coffee from large mugs
we wandered through sculptures
as big as cows

we read poems on the walls
we saw things which were like ghosts

we threw questions at each other
knew our own doubts
braved the possibilities

we sat on a long road
and thought nothing of it

i made a list
a poem list
a list like a poem

i can do these kinds of things

some people get me
some people don't

sometimes i'm the wrong order on a menu
sometimes i'm just a taste to get used to

sixty seven - not enough

too much electricity
not enough love

too much yammering inside
not enough of the good stuff

too much of that which isn't
not enough of the song which helps

too much of everything i don't need
not enough holding myself

too many words
not enough deliberate

too much numbness
not enough shine

let fizzle fizzle out and weep
let me walk and let me sleep

sixty eight - rattles

somehow through fallow steps – rain draws me out
cools me in its odd shift – not full but enough
to chill the waves of heat that've held me down
(recently sleep's only been the lack of waking up

and shaking myself from soft pillows of regret)
but here i am holding whatever key i can turn
into a lock – that's metaphor – and there it's said
my life's indeed a cage that shuts a bird

inside itself – but for now – rain's drawn me out
i follow where it goes – a fart that's rough
i know will do me positive – i sieve the drought
outside myself – finale's waking up

sun's done with me – shrunk me in my skin
rain's turn (and turn again) rattles in its tin

sixty nine - hear

i have had two days
of bad listening

these are words like

past - before
previously - gone
            should

i have been tried by
many such thoughts

other times
other shapes
other futures
have tried me also

i am present
i am myself
with challenges

this has happened
things will improve

see
hear
know

a is for akal

seventy - forever sometimes

infinity pre-empts a wide sunset
infinity draws out my yearning
                              my finding

infinity knows what i am like
-      weak mostly
-      scatter fashioned
-      always never
-      forever sometimes
-      day sleepy
-      a hint of sadness

infinity is brave for taking me on
infinity expects me to hold it like
          a large vase of flowers
it is too much
and i drop it
on its edge

when i try to catch infinity
i use soft gloves
          a large bag
          a hope of somehow

i have too many shadows to wrestle with

but
i hear others
i join in
i am ok

am ok

Thanks

Proof-readers: Frank, Niall and Rosie
Family and friends
The Word and Action community
Yoga and meditation tutor, Denise
Anne of publishers, Big White Shed

For more information about the writer, go to
www.nottinghamcommunityarts.blogspot.com

Cover illustration photographed by Jon Legge
https://jonleggephotography.blogspot.com